Never Annuitize

Never Annuitize

WHAT YOUR AGENT NEVER TOLD YOU

John Radjenovich Jr.

J Namdar Publishing

ISBN 10: 0692370811
ISBN 13: 9780692370810

Table of Contents

The Truth of the Matter (introduction)

How can you **avoid the trap** that has placed millions in a financial bind?

This booklet is dedicated to those life insurance companies and life insurance agents that want to provide what is right for the consumer.

If you are an insurance agent, wouldn't you want to do what's right for the consumer?

If you are a consumer, wouldn't you want your insurance agent to do what's right for your family?

NOTE: After enduring 20 years as an insurance school administrator, I feel quite qualified to share some startling facts about life insurance companies and their agents. Did I forget to mention that the school I operated was an insurance pre-licensing school to prepare "newbies" in the insurance arena to pass the test to become a "professional" agent?

Introduction

In this book I am not siding with anybody. I am attempting to educate the agents and protect the consumer.

This booklet is one of the most powerful tools ever orchestrated to help consumers make choices that will help their families financially. Never has this info been shared from the standpoint of a school that educated the agents.

For those of you that do remember and for those of you that are interested in history, let's take a trip back to the 1940s and 1950s. When a newborn entered the world, it was a "tradition" for the family to take out a $1000, $5000 or $10,000 life insurance policy on that addition to the family. Your agent buddy up the block would come over to share your happiness and depart after issuing your pride and joy a small whole life insurance plan that every child should have. Again, this was "tradition". The agent's job was selling insurance, and he/she knew nothing to be wrong with what they were doing. After all, the agents up to the 1970s-1980s did not have to attend a pre-licensing school. Their companies would supply adequate reading material for them to pass the state exam. Once passed, the agent became a "professional". The agent had a job.

In today's world the agent must take a class either classroom or online, depending on the state. After the class the agent studies to prepare for the state exam. From all observations the agent is better prepared to enter the life insurance arena. What the company allows the agent to pass on to the consumer is a different story. They sell what the company wants them to sell.

For as long as the insurance industry has been in existence, a way has been created to establish a means to greater profits for its companies and agents, allowing a trillion dollar industry to evolve. Americans from across the land fell and are falling into a trap. As changes occur, your insurance needs also have to be altered to the delight of those licking their chops, visualizing larger than life dollar signs. To this moment the average American finds the ready cash to fill those dreams, while their own are flushed away. (Agents are informed that certain products be pushed at the public to generate greater revenues for the company. Since changes are rapid, agents can't always be totally aware of the ramifications of their products, but, innocently, stride forward to milk the public). *After all, everyone's entitled to a fair income.*

To sell their company's products, many agents approach clients under the guise of an investment counselor, investment advisor or financial planner. (It's a way of getting their foot in the door). Some agents, actually, are certified to discuss investments and other finances with their clients. It is not out of the picture for a client to request to see the licenses held by an agent. (Agents are mandated to carry their licenses with them at all times when involved in sales presentations). So, as a client, don't hesitate to ask to see the licenses.

NOTE: At our Continuing Education classes it would amaze me that the vast majority of agents did not carry their licenses on their possession. Some had no idea where their licenses were.

Having been in the insurance education industry for twenty years I chuckle at the insurance ads on radio and television that refer to their agents as "professionals". (Maybe everyone that works in our world should be called a "professional"). When I was a youngster, I put in about as many hours training to sell ice cream on a motorized cart as agents put in to prepare for the life exam. I was never called a "professional". (Life insurance pre-licensing in my state mandates 20 hours of education). Enough said!

For the next day, week or month, try to see the light in a presently dark tunnel of the life insurance world, as presented by one who knows- your friendly agent and agent educator.

Choose Your Poison (Life Insurance)

1. Ordinary life
2. Traditional Life
3. Universal Life
4. Variable Life
5. Whole Life
6. Variable-Universal Life
7. Straight Life
8. Term Life
9. Annuities
10. Termanent Life *(or whatever other name is on your life insurance product)*

Now you are ready for the next leap.

View Your Policy

Take Out Your Policy
(It is OK to be ignorant; not knowing about something)

Having identified your present life insurance policy, try to convince yourself what you have is the product you need or the product your agent informed you is in the hands of an intelligent person for knowing his/her needs. Right? Wrong! As confusing as this paragraph is, your insurance policy is more confusing. Let me simplify the entire situation. Take out your policy, read it from cover to cover and ready yourself for the test that could place you in the upper 10% of the "ABC Insurance School" for your kind of life insurance policy. You probably would receive an acceptable score of 50% to earn that position in the school. The point at hand is ignorance- yours, mine, your neighbor's, Uncle Joe's, the milkman, to name a few. If I include myself in this group, you might wonder how such a booklet can be written by yours truly. (Twenty years of experience with the insurance school have helped me gain the tag "The Agent Guru"). With this in mind let's attack!

When students entered my classroom, I would first ask them to write down the spelling of 'Albuquerque'. (Maybe 10% of all students over the years spelled it correctly). What does this have to do with life insurance? I estimate that the same small percentage (10%) of policy holders know how their life insurance policy works and what type of policy they have. Since pre-licensing schools have entered the scene, agents are better educated, but consumers still fall into the less-informed category. Why? The following pages should shed some light on this matter.

What's Not In the Classroom Text?

The Written Text To Equip Life Agents With The Knowledge Needed To Pass The Exam

Yes, I was the culprit who created the "vultures" of this titanic industry. However, in my defense I presented the facts as they were written in our textbooks. Written by whom? Written by the "vultures" that possessed the expertise in the life insurance industry. Throughout the nation there are textbooks that contain the core of knowledge to pass the agent exams, assembled_by life insurance industry experts. What's not included on the state exam? Answer: "Not all of the facts!" Why not? All of the facts are *not* included in the pre-licensing textbooks; so why would they be included on the state exam.

NOTE: *Only what insurance companies want to be in the text and on the exam are included*

Let me site one example:

> One book that we utilized in our school classes had several pages that were **not numbered** relating to a given fact. It was perfect for our classes to have these unnumbered pages included because we wanted our students to know this particular fact.

If this same text were to be sold to another school, the author would leave out the unnumbered pages. Sounds sleazy!! It is! My guess is that 95% (might be higher) of all insurance school textbooks do not include this particular fact.

NOTE: Before I tell you about this fact I must state that insurance is divided into four basic categories: 1. Life; 2. Accident and Health; 3. Property; and 4. Casualty.

(My attack is on the life insurance phase of the industry- the most destructive phase that takes advantage of the vulnerability of the consumer without the consumer knowing it is happening).

What Happens to Your Cash Values?

The Misconception: Cash Values

Now let's get back to those unnumbered pages in the students' textbooks that are left out of over 95% (a logical assumption) of all life insurance textbooks. The fact? The fact is *"Cash Values"* in a life insurance policy **belong to the life insurance company**. This is a fact that companies do not want their agents to convey to their clients because informing the client of this fact would be a dagger in the sale. (Instead, companies train their agents to use cash values as a selling point when presenting their products). Just remember that cash values always belong to the insurance company. Sad to say, the agents pushing their company's products might not be aware of this. (It was not in their pre-licensing book; so how would they know).

NOTE: One of our first textbooks had several unnumbered pages that reminded the students no less than five (5) times 'Remember, cash values belong to the insurance company'.

Many of you might own a traditional cash value life insurance policy. Let me explain how it works:

Example #1   Policy Coverage: $100,000
> Premium is paid for this coverage ($83 per month)
> Cash value builds within the policy
> Death occurs
> Beneficiary receives death benefit of $100,000
> Company keeps the cash value

Example #2   Policy Coverage: $100,000
> Premium is paid for this coverage ($83 per month)
> Cash value builds within the policy
> Client decides to cancel policy
> Client takes out cash values
> Death benefit of $100,000 is terminated

NOTE: You never get both: the death benefit and the cash values; and I should also include that the beneficiary never gets both.

Cash value life insurance policies carry many titles. (I will bring back these throughout the booklet).

1. Ordinary life
2. Traditional Life
3. Permanent
4. Universal Life
5. Variable Life
6. Whole Life
7. Variable-Universal Life
8. Straight Life
9. Termanent Life *(or whatever other "creative" name is on your life insurance product)*

Just remember, if you possess one of these, your premium is paying for two (2) parts: death benefit (coverage) and cash value. However, the company will never pay out both.

The Proof Is In the Pudding/Borrowing Your Own Money

To prove who owns the cash value, when you need to take out some cash from your cash values to assist in a few bill payments, you must borrow the money and pay interest on the loan. Can you believe you have to borrow "your" money? You do! What a farce! The agent sells you on the point that you have coverage and cash value building within the policy. Did he tell you that you have to borrow the cash that you assumed was yours? Why would he? It wasn't in the textbook, and it wasn't on the exam.

One nice thing about borrowing the cash value is that you don't have to pay it back. How does the company get "their" cash value back? When you die, your beneficiary will receive the death benefit (coverage) minus any cash value that was borrowed and not paid back. (You don't ever have to feel sorry for an insurance company. They will cover every angle to win the cash battle).

So, why are you paying for both? Look no further! That smooth talking friendly agent is a trained "steamroller". He possesses answers to cover every base. (In most cases he is a friend of yours. Would a friend take advantage of you? If he is a Life Insurance agent, I would say "Yes!"). Am I showing some strong convictions? You bet I am!

Is life Insurance
An Investment?

Life Insurance: Is it an investment? *What a joke!*

New life insurance policies are disguised to look like an "investment". The only Life insurance product that is considered an investment is an annuity. To reiterate, annuities are the only insurance products that are investments. (No matter what the agent says, life insurance is not an investment).

Variable life insurance is a relatively new insurance program that allows the client to place the cash values into a mixed array of stock choices. (Many ill-informed agents claim that it is the same as buying term life insurance and investing in mutual funds). Wrong! *Just remember who owns the cash value. You are the "picker" of the investment choices, and the company is the "keeper" of the funds.*

There are Dividends and Then There are Dividends

What Are Dividends In Life Insurance Policies?
Not what you think!

Have you witnessed television and radio commercials by insurance companies that brag that they have paid out billions in dividends over the years to their policyholders? Hopefully, you are aware of them. They are very powerful commercials that depict companies giving so much back to their life insurance policyholders. (I get sick when I hear or view those commercials. They are true cases of misrepresenting the term 'dividend'. Let me explain).

In the minds of investors a dividend is a payback to the shareholder due to the stock company's excellent sales performance during the year. Wonderful! *Isn't it the same with dividends in life insurance policies?* No! No! No!

In a life insurance policy dividends are paid on policies that have the words "participating" or "dividend paying" located on the bottom of your first policy page under the type of insurance program you possess (lower left side of front page): *'Whole Life- participating' or 'Variable Life- dividend paying'*

If your policy does not pay dividends, you might see "non-participating" after the type of policy: *'Whole Life- non-participating'*

So, what is a dividend in a life insurance policy? Simply stated, it is a <u>partial return of an overcharge</u> of your premium (U.S. Treasury

Decision Number 1743). Yes! The company overcharges you for your policy, and it will return some of that overcharge if it does not need all of it to fund a new building, give raises to their executives, purchase a new jet, or for any other item that benefits the company-not you. Who owns the largest buildings in your community?

Let me site this example:

> Your premium- $1500 annually
> Your true life insurance cost- $1200 annually
> You were overcharged $300
> At the end of the year the company sends you $100
> That $100 is your "dividend"
> (You were overcharged $300 and returned $100).
> Sounds like a plan! Remember: A dividend in a life insurance policy is a partial return of an overcharge of your premium.

Should companies be bragging about the billions paid back in dividends to their policyholders? They are preying on the ignorance (not knowing what a life insurance dividend is) of people and misleading people to believe that their policy dividends are the same as investment dividends. No! No! No! If they are paying back billions of dollars in "dividends", how much have they overcharged their policyholders? Perhaps trillions?

Keep in mind that a life insurance dividend is "a partial return of an overcharge of premiums".

> **Headlines: "Company ABC" will pay 10% interest on dividends"**. Imagine that! You get $100 + $10 = $110 as your total, and you were overcharged $300. How deceptive!

Review: So far, you are aware of 2 very important deceptions by the life insurance industry. Cash values and dividends are used by agents and companies as "selling points" to "snow" their clients.

Dividends: What Do I Do With Them? (Hopefully, you aren't in this position)

Remember that we have already discussed what dividends are: **a partial return of an overcharge** of premiums (your payment for coverage of life insurance).

Let's discuss what you can do with your dividends (partial return of your overcharge). An acronym can help you remember this info: CARP. *(Perhaps you can create a better acronym!)*

C- Cash   You can receive a check from the company and go out for a fish fry or dinner.

A-Accumulated   You can allow the dividends to stay pat and accumulate within the policy.

R- Reduced   You can use the dividends to apply towards your premiums.

P- Paid up   You can purchase additional paid-up life insurance.

NOTE: *Interest on the dividends is taxable. (Can you believe that!)*

Life or Death Insurance?

Life Insurance? Do I Need It?

Yes, you do! But it should be called "Death Insurance". You need life insurance to protect your family and your income in case of premature death. That is the main reason for life insurance. Protect your family! Protect your family! Protect your family!

Do you need life insurance forever? The industry wants you to believe you do. That's why whole life was created. As soon as a newborn comes into the world, it's time to give him/her a "gift" of life insurance; hence, whole life begins at age zero and can, also, begin at any other age. When does it end? The life insurance people decided 100 years was a perfect ending for whole life insurance. So, the "perfect" whole life policy extends from age zero to age 100.

If you have a $50,000 cash value whole life policy, it will endow at age 100. Endow means that the policy will fully mature. The cash value will equal the death benefit. So, if you are 100 years old, it would behoove you to keep the policy any longer. Cash in your policy and receive $50,000 in cash from the company. (Time to go out and have a fling). Remember how old you are: 100.

Now that didn't take long! Only 100 years. (I wonder what percent of people that owned whole life policies actually cashed them in at age 100). Remember, you will never receive both the cash value and the death benefit.

If you read no further, you will have become quite knowledge-able about the whole life industry and how the whole life policy operates. Reading further you will become aware of many pitfalls that can be avoided.

How Does That Annuity Work?

Annuities: The Only Life Insurance Product That Is An Investment

Annuities are the only life insurance products that are investment tools of a life insurance company. (No matter what an agent tells you, remember that annuities are life insurance products). Annuities are not mutual funds, but insurance companies can sell mutual funds to their clients in addition to annuities.

There are two kinds of annuities: 1) fixed and 2) variable. To sell fixed annuities an agent only needs a life insurance license. To sell variable annuities an agent needs a life insurance license and a Series 6 license (a securities license to sell variable annuities, mutual funds and variable life insurance).

Now the fun begins! Your agent approaches you with a "double-barreled rifle"- life insurance with cash value and an annuity. His goal, ultimately, is to make money for the company and himself. What is the best way to accomplish that feat? First, and utmost in his mind, is to collar you with a life insurance policy that has coverage and cash value. Once you are hog-tied with such a plan the agent convinces you of a need for an investment (the annuity). All finalized with your cash in his hand the agent departs with a handshake and a huge smile on his face- all the way to the bank.

He has just milked you of all he could. Don't feel badly! Truckloads of Americans have met with a similar fate. (What should the agent have presented and sold to you? Pure life insurance (term) and a separate investment). Remember how a cash value life insurance policy operates? Who owns the cash value?

To remedy your situation of owning a whole life policy and an annuity, you must take matters into your own hands.

1rst Step: Don't sell anything, and don't cancel anything.

2nd Step: Find a company that only offers term life (pure) insurance. (Some do exist!) Suggestion: Don't go back to your "friendly" agent. He just took advantage of you and your family. Term is pure insurance- no cash value or dividends. (Similar in design to homeowners and auto insurance- pure coverage with no cash value attached).

3rd Step: Buy an appropriate amount of term life insurance. (It will be based on your income, age and family size).

4th Step: Find an investment company. ("ABC Stocks", "Mom's Mutual Funds", "XYZ Investments") After reading this booklet should your investments be with an insurance company?. Feel comfortable with your selection.

5th Step: Select your investment. My choice is always a mutual fund that invests with growth companies. (There are many other options available).

6th Step: *Determine what you can invest per month*. You can calculate the amount by looking at the premium you are paying for your current life insurance policy with cash values plus the money you are placing into your annuity and then subtracting the cost of your new term life program.

Example:	Old Plan	$200 per month for you cash value whole life policy
		+$100 per month into your annuity
	New Plan	-$75 per month for your new term life program
		=*$225 per month available to invest in your growth mutual fund*

7th Step: Create your **monthly** investment plan in a growth mutual fund. Suggestion: Place the investment in a **Roth IRA** (no taxes when withdrawals are taken at retirement) **growth mutual fund**. (Some people prefer to pay taxes when they retire and opt for a traditional IRA).

8th Step: After your new term life policy is in effect (approved and issued), cancel your previous life policy with cash values.

9th Step: Freeze your annuity- no further monies to be placed in the annuity. Your new investment company and you can decide what to do with it later. (New monies will enter your new mutual fund plan).

Let's assume that you keep your current annuity with no further funds going into it. We will give it a value of $15,000 and call it a variable annuity. When you are ready to retire, you will have a value of $60,000 in this annuity- after 30 years- about 4.5% per year growth.

Now let's assume one more thing. The growth mutual fund that you are investing in ($225 per month) and calling a Roth IRA grows to $1,000,000.

If you had placed the monthly amount in the variable annuity, it could have grown to $1,000,000 at your retirement. (So, why did we make the change 30 years earlier?)

To gain full understanding, let's look at the options.

Annuities: The Options (and the mistake that you might make)

Your mistake, shall you decide to make it at retirement, will cost you a mere $60,000. (Remember: your annuity grew to $60,000 after 30 years).

What mistake?

With an annuity you have three options: 1) leave it untouched to continue to grow; 2) take it all out; or 3) take a monthly payout. Because you are retired, your friendly agent will lead you to option #3- take a monthly payout. After all, your payout of an annuity is taxable. Would you want the entire $60,000 added to your income and be taxed at a higher rate, or would you rather spread out the dollars monthly over your entire lifetime and keep the tax rate at a lower rate? Most of those offered the choice select the "spreading out" plan (called annuitizing)- taking out a fixed monthly amount for the remainder of one's life.

That's the Mistake!

When you annuitize (select a monthly payout for your lifetime) you "give" the $60,000, in this case, to the insurance company. The money enters their pool. The money no longer belongs to you. It belongs to the company!

You possess a contract that pays you a monthly payout until you die- about 4% per year of your original amount ($2400 a year until you die).

Imagine if you had kept socking away money into the annuity over the past 30 years, and the value grew to $1,000,000, and you selected the monthly payout option, **you would have made a $1,000,000 mistake.** (For the rest of your lifetime you would receive about $40,000 a year. The amount cannot be changed once you annuitize). Remember where the $1,000,000 goes? It goes into the insurance company's pool of cash and belongs to the insurance company.

That's why you made the change 30 years earlier!

Again, the mistake becomes more obvious when you view your growth mutual fund that is called a Roth IRA growth mutual fund. Your fund is worth $1,000,000 at retirement. (Let's start having some fun!) 4% per year- $40,000 annually- is taken from your account. The remainder, $960,000 plus, silently awaits your next withdrawal. The money belongs to you at all times- unlike the annuity. Because you labeled it a Roth IRA no taxes are ever paid on withdrawals. You can change your monthly withdrawals- unlike the annuity. You are in total control!

If you have an annuity, I know you won't make "the mistake" after reading this booklet.

To phrase a former client's wife: 'What does never annuitize mean? I found your card in my husband's belongings. *Never annuitize!! Never annuitize!! Never annuitize!!* was printed on the card.'

If you follow those words, you can never make "the mistake".

Remember what you did with your annuity when you retired? You decided to take a monthly withdrawal for the rest of your life and turned over the principal to the insurance company. Good-bye principal! You **annuitized** your annuity (accepted a monthly withdrawal from the company).

My definition of annuitize: to allow the life insurance company to "steal" your money and in exchange offer you a paltry monthly payout until you die.

Never allow that to happen!

Annuities: Payouts (once you made "the mistake" or you possess a retirement plan that only allows you to annuitize)

The first part of "the mistake" is opting to take a monthly payout, and the second part of the mistake is signing the contract that confirms that decision. You have "gifted" your entire retirement to the insurance company. You will never see or touch that money again. The company thanks you for making "the mistake".

Now that you annuitized, do you know what plan you chose?

The highest paid monthly payout is called **Straight Life Annuity Payout.** It might pay out $3000 a year on your $60,000 annuity. A lower paying program called **10-Year Period Certain Annuity Payout** might pay out $2400 a year. Why the difference? One is riskier than the other and offers no payments to your beneficiary.

NOTE: There are many other options; however, these two give you an idea of the most risky to a less risky payout.

> **Straight Life Payout**- The moment you die the payments end.

10-Year Period Certain Payout- Pays out for a minimum of 10 years (to you until you die and to your beneficiary for up to 10 years if you die before the 10-year period passes).

How about your neighbor? He just retired- 65 years old- and has a $1,000,000 annuity. He goes to the office of the "XYZ Insurance Company" and annuitizes- selects a monthly payment contract and signs the contract. He opts for the highest payout plan- The **Straight Life Payout** plan. A month later he receives his first monthly payment from "XYZ Company" for $4000. A week later he falls off his horse, strikes his head on a tree and dies. After much grieving the wife stops by "XYZ Company" to see what will happen with the remainder of the $1,000,000. (No matter who you are it is hard to hide greed). The husband's "keeper of the funds" informs the widow that the **Straight Life Payout** option was selected by her husband and pays out until the husband's death; hence no further payments will be made. What about the $1,000,000? (Remember what happens when you annuitize and sign a contract for a monthly payout. The $1,000,000 goes into the "XYZ Company" pool and stays there. It belongs to the company. After all, they are the "keeper" of the funds). The husband selected the most risky payout option, and his widow paid dearly for it.

How does an agent inform the grieving widow that the $1,000,000 is not hers? (No honor among thieves!)

Had the husband selected the 10-Year Period Certain Payout, the widow would continue to receive $3000 a month payments for the remainder of the 10 years.

Now the numbers might be a bit out of line; but the greed shows.
Never Annuitize! Never Annuitize! Never Annuitize!

Annuities: A Salvage Plan

How can you salvage your annuity? Remember your plan? You found an investment firm that handled your mutual fund. He can help you transfer the annuity into a mutual fund. (Once you transfer the money from the annuity to a mutual fund, you become the owner. You have "rescued" your money).

Had you annuitized your annuity could you transfer the money to a mutual fund? No!! No!! No!! Just remember: Never Annuitize!!

NOTE: Government workers, state retirements and some corporations are the exceptions. At retirement the only option might be to annuitize.

NOTE: A new kind of annuity has been created by the industry that allows the person to take out a monthly payout on his/her life until death. *If* any money is left in that account at death, it will be passed on to the beneficiary.

Life Insurance: The Beneficiary (Remember not to annuitize)

Certain times in your lifetime a family member will pass on. You might be the beneficiary of a life insurance policy. If so, the agent will endeavor to have you "annuitize" the death benefit. Say 'No thank you!' and take the lump sum. Death proceeds are not taxable in most cases. There could be an estate tax if the numbers mandate it. (Just take the lump sum and invest it with your investment advisor).

Why So Many Different Kinds of Life Insurance?

Life Insurance: The Different Types (the Good, the Bad and the Ugly)

Cash value life insurance policies carry many titles.

1. Ordinary life
2. Traditional Life
3. Universal Life
4. Variable Life
5. Whole Life
6. Straight Life
7. Permanent Life
8. Termanent Life *(or whatever other "creative" name is on your life insurance product)*

First of all, why so many different names? Good question! **Ordinary Life, Traditional Life, Straight Life, Permanent Life and Whole Life** possess the same meaning and are the names for the basic cash value life insurance plans.

> Basic cash value whole life guarantees: death benefit, cash values and fixed premium

Universal Life is a cash value plan that is very flexible (no guarantees). **What a beauty!**

Guarantees: none

Variable Life is a cash value plan where cash values are invested in a variety of investments.

Guarantees: death benefit (can be less than the amount shown on the front of the policy)

Termanent Life is a created name for a cash value plan (somewhat deceptive). One might believe that he owns a term life plan (the only pure life insurance plan). During my days as an agent, I came across this Termanent Life policy. (I have never seen another one since then). Even the internet searches can only find permanent plans when you look up 'Termanent Life'.

Before I delve into some of the plans above I want you to know that all plans start with pure insurance, and cash value programs are added on. If you buy pure insurance (term), no cash value plans are included. *(Consumerists that are not attached to life insurance companies recommend term life insurance).*

Universal Life Insurance is my favorite plan to pick on. As stated above, it is flexible with no guarantees. To start off, I am going to put you on a plane with 100 of your clones. All 100 of your clones will be sold the same Universal Life Insurance plan by the same agent and contain the same death benefit ($250,000). The policies have been in effect for a year. Here's where the flexibility comes in. Clone #1 pays an annual premium of $200; Clone # 2 pays an annual premium of $300; Clone #3 pays an annual premium of $400 and so on up to Clone #100 who pays an annual premium of $10,000. The plane crashes, and all clones die. What does each of the 100 beneficiaries receive as a death benefit? $250,000! Clone #1 paid an annual premium of $200, and Clone #100 paid an annual premium of $10,000. No matter what premium was paid the death benefit was the same. The agent sold all 100 the same policy with the same death benefit.

Remember that this is a cash value plan. Those paying the lower premiums had little or no cash value build-up in their policies. Those paying the higher premiums would have some cash value building up.

Let's assume the plane landed safely and did not crash, and a period of 10 years passes. (Again remember the policies are identical. The differences are found in the premium paid by each clone.)

Clone #1 was paying a premium of $200. Each year for the last nine years he received a letter stating that an additional premium must be paid to keep the current death benefit or keep paying the same premium and maintain a lower death benefit. Clone #1 opted to pay the same premium of $200 for the next nine years and has a current death benefit of $20,000. (A far cry from the original death benefit of $250,000.) *This is flexibility!*

Clone #2 was paying a premium of $300. For the last seven years he received the same letter that Clone #1 received. Clone #2 opted to keep the same death benefit ($250,000) and is currently paying a premium of $800. (What's the premium going to be in another ten years?) *This is flexibility!*

Clone #3 was paying a premium of $400. After three years he received the same letter as Clones #1 and #2. He no longer is in the program. *This is flexibility!*

Clones #4, #5 and #6 also received the same letter. One has a higher premium; another has a lower death benefit; and the third has dropped out of the plan. Will they be in the plan in another ten years? (No Way!) *This is flexibility!*

As time passes the clones paying the lower premiums will have to make the same decisions. *This is flexibility!*

As presented earlier all policies begin with pure insurance (term), and a cash value plan can be added. In the case with a Universal Life Insurance policy each year the cost of the term life goes up. If the cash values in your Universal Life plan are depleted (gone with the wind), you will receive "the letter".

Let's assume that Clone #15 currently is paying a premium of $1600 annually. He has a cash value accumulation of $5500. When will he receive "the letter"? My guess is in a few years.

Clone #100, paying a premium of $10,000 annually, may or may not receive "the letter". *This is flexibility!*

How many of the 100 will be in this program after 15years; 20 years; or 25 years?

NOTE: The Universal Life Insurance policy has no guarantees!

How about taking a quick glance at the **Variable Life Insurance** plan. What makes it different from other plans is the cash value plan offered to you. In all other cash value plans you have no say as to where the cash values go. In the Variable Life policy you have the opportunity to select where the cash values go. (Big Deal!) *Remember who owns the cash values! The company owns the cash values. If you want to take some out, you must borrow the cash, proving, once again, that the company owns the cash values.*

The Variable Life policy has one guarantee. If you keep paying the requested premium, you will have a death benefit. (What is that death benefit? It could be the same as specified on the front page of your policy or less).

NOTE: One of my instructors argued that the life insurance industry has created a policy that pays out both death benefit and cash values upon death. He could not offer proof in any policy that states you get both. What policies do state: 'Upon death the beneficiary will receive a death benefit equal to the face amount of the policy and the cash values.' (Monies are taken out of the cash values over the years to purchase additional life insurance; hence the new face amount will equal the original face value of the policy and the cash values). It sure looks like you are getting both!

As for **Traditional Whole Life**, everything is guaranteed. It is the original whole life that was created with pure life insurance (term) and a cash value account. It has a set premium. It has a set death benefit. It has a set cash value chart. All three are guaranteed to remain constant. If you are looking to protect your family upon your premature death, this will be extremely expensive if you desire to purchase the appropriate amount of coverage.

NOTE: All cash value accounts are classified as permanent insurance. Pure life insurance claims the title of term insurance. (The vast majority of life insurance in force is permanent insurance). Why? Our ignorance!

With time the life insurance industry "lab" develops new names and slight changes in a permanent plan (life coverage with cash values) to introduce to their clients. Just remember any cash value life policy possesses the same basics we have discussed throughout this booklet. No matter what the agent tells you about this new "to good to be true" life policy, make certain you remember the basics. You will be saved at every turn if you follow that advice.

As stated earlier the life insurance industry has created a product that claims your beneficiary will receive both the death benefit and the cash values upon your death. Remember the unnumbered pages in the class textbook stating 'the cash values belong to the insurance company'. (Don't you ever forget that statement!)

It is important that this be repeated. If you are approached by an agent selling this product, you should ask him to bring in a policy that says "the beneficiary will receive the death benefit **and** the cash values" upon death. (In the years that I ran the school I confronted many agents about that statement. None could show me what I had requested). What the policy states is that the beneficiary will receive an **amount equivalent** to the death benefit and the cash values. It does not say the beneficiary receives the death benefit and the cash values. What the company does to increase the death benefit is to take out a portion of your cash values to buy enough additional life insurance to bring the death benefit up to the original death benefit and the cash values.

Simply explained in this hypothetical example:
(Both plans start out with a death benefit of $200,000)
Traditional Plan
After 3 years Death Benefit $200,000   Cash Values   2,128
Type II Plan (death benefit increases)
After 3 years Death Benefit $202,017   Cash Values   2,017

Note the differences in cash values. Looking at the cash values, the company has used $111 of the cash values from a traditional plan to buy an additional amount of life insurance ($2,017) for the Type II plan; hence the death benefit is equivalent to the original death benefit and the cash values. If you were to get both, the death benefit would be $202,017 + $2017= $204,034. *JUST REMEMBER: YOU NEVER GET THE CASH VALUES WHEN DEATH OCCURS!*

If you were to cancel the Type II Plan after 3 years, what would you receive from the life insurance company? Surprise! The $2017 in cash values would be your "reward".

What is a Viatical or Who is the Viatical?

Viatical Settlement Companies (The "Pawn Shop" of the Industry)

NOTE: I am not sure if they exist anymore; but they were included in our textbooks. Should they still be around would shock me.

Viatical settlement companies were **created** to offer viatical services to their clients.

What is a viatical service?

> Definition: An agreement in which a person with a terminal illness sells his or her life insurance policy for immediate cash (less than the death benefit/face value). The purchaser cashes in the policy when the original owner dies.

If a client has a terminal illness and wants to do something special prior to death, the company would offer that client 30-80% cash on a valid life insurance policy prior to death. The client has to prove that the terminal illness exists, and the percent of cash payout is based on a variety of conditions. The viatical settlement company would become the beneficiary of the valid life insurance policy by purchasing the policy. (This is another way the company takes your money). It is a service!

Let me site an example:

> Client has a valid life insurance policy
> $200,000 death benefit
> Has terminal cancer
> Expected to live 6 months to a year (doctor's confirmation)
> Viatical Settlement Company purchases the policy and gives the client $80,000 cash immediately
> Client dies 8 months later
> Company receives the $200,000 death benefit as the beneficiary (owner of the policy)

There are life insurance companies that will offer clients 30-40% cash prior to death on a policy for a confirmed terminal illness and deduct that cash from the death benefit when paying out the monies to the designated beneficiary (spouse, parent, son, daughter, friend, church). This is fine. The company is not receiving your death benefit.

Family and friends should be the recipients of your death benefit. Why not ask them for the cash and make them the beneficiary of your policy. Stay away from the "pawn shop" if they are still out there.

"Life" Can Be Wonderful

What Should I Do With My "Life"

Some facts to be aware of with Life Insurance:

1. Each policy has a policy fee and administrative charges; so you should have one policy that covers the entire family. (I came across a family that had 13 different life insurance policies with four different companies). Whoa!

2. Watch out for "add-ons"(options). You will frequently come across flyers in the mail that offer a high death benefit ($500,000 coverage) for a small fee per year ($107). Usually, it is an accidental death policy that is payable if you die due to an accident. If you add an accidental death clause to your life insurance policy, an additional fee is charged.

   (NOTE: If you have accidental death coverage, and if you are involved in an accident and taken to the hospital, you cannot die from other causes while in the hospital to collect the accidental death benefit. Having a heart attack in the hospital which results in death voids the accidental death option. Also, there is a stipulated timeframe during which the death must occur. If that timeframe is 3 months, you cannot die from the accident after 3 months in order to have an accidental death payout.)

3. Life insurance on children? Why? (Remember the "tradition"? Forget tradition!) When a child is born, he/she

is either insurable or uninsurable. Why is life insurance so "cheap" at young ages? Answer: Insurance companies know that insurable children are going to live a long and prosperous life. *(NOTE: age 40 is when life insurance fees start the upward movement. Death is beginning to surface).*

4. How many times have you received info from your mortgage company suggesting that you purchase mortgage insurance on your home? *Mortgage insurance is life insurance!* If you have adequate term life insurance coverage, you do not need mortgage insurance. (It's another policy and another fee!) *NOTE: The same is true with Credit Life (on purchasing a car or other major items).* If you have adequate term life insurance coverage, you do not need credit life insurance.

"Life" should be simple! It is, if you follow a plan. To conclude:

1. Always buy pure life insurance (term) to protect your family
2. Buy adequate life insurance coverage (6 to 8 times your income)
3. Invest monthly in a growth mutual fund (call it a Roth IRA)
4. Never annuitize
5. Beware of the agent that does not present all of the facts
6. There are agents out there that promote what's best for you and your family. Do some digging to find one.

Let me extend my congratulations to you for completing this booklet. Follow through with the knowledge that I have bestowed upon you, and you and your family will reap the rewards over your lifetimes.

If you follow this plan, you will avoid the traps of financial doom that were stressed throughout this book.

__Suggested Readings__ (classics of caring consumerists from the past)

Money Dynamics by Venita Van Caspel/ Life Insurance: Still the Great National Consumer Dilemma

Straight Talk by Oliver W. Horsman

All You Can Do is All You Can Do by A.L. Williams

What's Wrong with Your Life Insurance by Norman F. Dacey

Life Insurance Cost Disclosure by Federal Trade Commission

Games and Scams of Life Insurance by Dr. Robert Pepin

U.S. Treasury Decision Number 1743

This question (dividends) was argued at great length and in full detail before the Internal Revenue Department and before Congress during the early months of 1911. The income tax clause of the Tarill Bill of 1911 proposed an income tax on Life Insurance Dividends. Representatives of companies featuring participating Insurance vigorously protested against this tax. The arguments and contentions of these companies are clearly set forth in the following quotations from UNITED STATES TREASURY DECISION NO. 1743:

"Reduced to final analysis the contentions of the various companies are…

"That dividends declared by participating companies are <u>not dividends in a commercial sense</u> of the word, <u>but are simply refunds to the policyholder of a portion of the overcharge collected,</u> which overcharge is merely held in trust by the company issuing the policy. Annually, or at stated periods, all, or a portion thereof, is returned to the person holding the policy…

It was vigorously contended by counsel, representing certain of these companies that it was necessary at the outset to disregard entirely the policy contracts, the published literature, the representatives of officers and agents, the sworn returns of state authorities, and to consider the proposition only after items had been eliminated: that owing to the urgent need of business and the competition of Insurance companies, <u>it was necessary. In order to secure new business to convince the prospective policyholder of the desirability of the same, and that this commercial necessity had resulted in the companies making misrepresentations of facts as to DIVIDENDS</u> to prospective purchasers of insurance, and that names and designations, having a single specific meaning in the commercial world and which were therefore attractive to prospective policyholders, had been adopted to represent transactions which they now hold are entirely different from what their name implies and represents, and from which the policyholder himself believed he was receiving, and that business necessities had caused a continuance of these misnomers. It was represented that, in fact, there were no dividends, <u>but merely a refund of overcharges</u>, which, for reasons above stated, were usually referred to as dividends."

In this connection, it is interesting to note how life insurance dividends are referred to in the present Federal Income Tax Regulation 94. In article 22, on Gross Income, Regulation 94, this statement appears: 'Amounts received as a return of premiums paid under life insurance, endowment, or annuity contracts, and so-called DIVIDENDS of a mutual insurance company which may be credited against the current premium, are not subject to tax.'"

Made in the USA
Middletown, DE
16 March 2021